Praise for *Starting Small*

Ben is not only a trusted friend, he's a trusted ministry advisor. One of Ben's greatest strengths is the ability to learn and then help others learn. He's done that for me many times. That's also why I'm happy to see Ben write this book. If you want to know small groups, there's no one I'd trust more to learn from than Ben. This will become known as a great resource for the Kingdom.

Ron Edmondson
Lead pastor, Immanuel Baptist Church
Organizational Leadership Consultant and Author at RonEdmondson.com

With the precision of a surgeon, the communication skills of a seasoned author, the humor of a stand up comedian, the biblical understanding of a veteran teaching pastor, and the passion of a man whose vision is to change the world through small groups, Ben unearths how to birth and oversee a healthy and flourishing small group ministry... in such a concise way. Wanna know what book I'll be suggesting to first time small group pastors...? You're holding it in your hand right now.

Rick Howerton
Small Group Specialist at Lifeway Christian Resources
Author of *A Different Kind of Tribe: Embracing the New Small Group Dynamics*

Ben takes us back to the heart of Small Group Ministry, the people. Ben has an ability for bringing out the basics of Small Group Ministry in a relational way. In *Starting Small* you will learn, or be reminded, how to launch and guide a ministry, a group, a movement to help people take their next step of faith.

Eddie Mosley
Executive Pastor of Group Life at Life Point Church
Author of *Connecting in Communities*

Ben Reed is not only one of the premier small group thinkers around, but he is also a practitioner. Through personal stories of successes and failures, this book will inspire both church leaders who are just exploring the idea of small groups, and seasoned group leaders that are looking for new inspiration. I highly recommend Starting Small for anyone that believes in circles over rows.

Chris Surratt
Pastor of Ministries
Cross Point Church, Nashville, TN

Starting Small

The Ultimate Small Group Blueprint

Ben Reed

© Copyright 2013
By Ben Reed
All Rights Reserved

Published by Rainer Publishing

To Laura, Rex, and Gracie Kate, my family.

You're the small group I love the most. I couldn't
have written this without you.

My heart is forever changed, and I'm better because
of you.

Contents

Foreword

Having done small groups for over 25 years, the last 15+ years at Saddleback Church, I meet a lot of small group pastors from all over the world. So when you meet someone with that raw talent, humble character, and submission to God you take notice. I first met Ben at a gathering of small group guys in 2008. The other guys in the room were a bunch of old friends of mine. Ben was the anomaly.

First of all, I didn't know him. I went *way back* with pretty much everyone else there. We had history, stories, and too many battle scares! But Ben and I didn't.

Second, he was years younger than everyone else. By at least a decade. He could have been any one of the guys kid! And somehow he'd weaseled his way to the table. I knew I had to get to know this guy.

It was when he cracked a joke...on me...that I knew this was a guy I could hang out with.

Ben and I hit it off, and now we talk every week about life, ministry, and groups. And in the process of talking through it all, Ben and I have become friends.

Ben's written a book here that you'll find *helpful*. When you read this book, it's like you're sitting down over a cup of coffee with Ben. It's like you've asked him, "Hey

Ben, can you help me think about small groups?" And instead of giving you a thick, dense, hard-to-understand manifesto about discipleship, he speaks in language that's accessible. Language that even a guy like me can understand!

It doesn't matter where you're at with small groups in your context. Maybe you're curious about how to get them started. Maybe you want to take them to the next level. Maybe you're a Sunday school fanatic. Or maybe you lead a house church. You'll appreciate this book!

Whether you're a small group veteran or a rookie, this book will help you think practically about raising the bar for your church's small group strategy. You'll be encouraged and challenged. I think you'll enjoy the ride.

I'm proud of the work Ben's done in *Starting Small*. This book will help your church; it has mine!

So sit down. Grab a cup of coffee. And enjoy a conversation with my friend.

Steve Gladen
Small Groups Pastor at Saddleback Church
Author of *Small Groups With Purpose* and *Leading Small Groups With Purpose*

Chapter 1

Introduction

I knew I loved ministry, just not the kind of ministry I was doing.

I was balancing several areas of my life: going to seminary, working as a barista in a local coffee shop, ministering as a youth pastor in a small, quaint church, and being a faithful husband. I quickly realized which of the four I didn't want to continue for the rest of my life (I still love to learn, I'm still married, and I am a coffee nut). It wasn't that I was terrible at pastoring young people. Or that I didn't see the value in it. I just found that my passions weren't ignited working with students. I just found myself continually drawn toward working with adults. And continually fired up when I was given the chance to speak into the lives of adults.

I preached. Organized trips. Counseled students. Led them to an understanding of Jesus. And we made some hay. The whole time, I knew there was a part of me that wasn't doing what God had prepared me to do. Not out of a heart of disobedience as much as a heart that was searching.

My wife and I were looking to make our way back towards middle Tennessee, knowing we wanted to start a family soon. Both of our parents lived in the Nashville area. God was working in my life, and the love for student ministry was fading. When I got the call from a church plant in my hometown, I was ready to jump. But the position was "small groups director." To which my first question was, "What's a small group?"

The process that propelled me to the "yes" involved exploring my own faith journey. I grew up in church. My parents made sure someone kept our seat warm in the worship center while they slipped away to the hospital to give birth to me. From an early age, I trusted Jesus. But it wasn't in the traditional church programs that God worked most beautifully and efficiently in my life. It wasn't in the preaching. Not through camps. Not through dynamic worship. Not through individual study. Though each of those left me marked, it was through a small group of guys that met together each week to study the Scriptures and engage each other on the things that mattered most. In this small group that met every Friday night (you can imagine how popular this made us with the ladies), we laughed, cried, yelled, studied, encouraged, ate, corrected, and wrestled (we were in high school). God changed me in ways I'd never been changed before. I began to understand and apply the Scriptures in fresh ways. I began to understand who it was God had created me to be.

Healthy, authentic, vulnerable, Christ-centered

community had propelled my spiritual growth like no other engine. God used it to spur me, and everyone in our group, to know and live the gospel in a more life-encompassing way. But in the moment, I didn't realize how vital it was. And as our group disassembled to go to colleges across the United States, I slowly but surely forgot about this aspect of faith. I didn't abandon relationships. I just abandoned the intentionality of them, settling for versions of community much safer.

When I began to minister through small groups, I had much to learn about the mechanics of small groups and how the system works in a church. But I fully understood the heart. Because I was living proof that it worked. My story was forever changed through healthy community. I was different because God used *intentional* relationships in a small group to bring change in my heart in a way that was much faster than other ways.

Maybe you're in a boat similar to mine. You know the value of small groups. God has used them in your life to help you grow. You've seen others impacted as they've chosen to live in healthy, authentic, Christ-honoring community. Maybe you've even led a small group or two yourself, whether in an official church capacity or in an off-the-radar capacity that wasn't officially sanctioned by the church. Maybe you just intuitively knew you needed others who were headed in the same direction. So you met.

Sometimes you studied a specific book. Sometimes you just laughed and prayed together. You didn't necessarily realize it in the moment, but looking back, you see just how important that weekly appointment was in your life. At the time, you knew you needed it. You just didn't know how much you needed it. And how much you would miss it once everyone had gone their separate ways and you were left sipping your blended coffee beverage by yourself.

The purpose of this book is to help you replicate that environment for others. How do you recreate the experience you had for an entire church? It takes a system to produce disciples, churn out leaders, and compel people to be on mission together. This book will help you through the process of putting this system together.

Is it even *possible* to recreate that experience for others? Or is the whole thing just so organic that we're just supposed to trust God, pray, and hope it will just happen with others? Is it possible to have a system that creates environments where life change is optimal, and where you can make the claim, "Join a small group and God will change your life?"

What I experienced in that influential small group felt simple and easy. It didn't feel forced or fake. It felt like a natural extension of your life and journey with Jesus. So why do we make it so complicated for others?

We make it so difficult because we assume that a group has to do more. Meet more often. Study more books. Talk more. Think more. Digest more.

The answer isn't in adding more and more burdens on small groups. It's in freeing small groups to do the right things in the right ways. Giving people a chance to meet the Jesus you know in a safe, predictable environment.

It is possible to recreate that amazing experience you had for others. You just need to take a wide-angle approach.

Are you ready? How has God worked most efficiently and effectively in your life to make you look more like Jesus? What part has small groups played?

If you don't know where your story intersects with small groups, it'll be hard for you to lead others to get excited. As we progress through these questions, you will discover how small groups can be a place where people *belong* so they can *become*.

Chapter 2

The Why before the What

"And let us consider how we may spur one another on toward love and good deeds, not giving up meeting together, as some are in the habit of doing, but encouraging one another—and all the more as you see the Day approaching."
Hebrews 10:24-25

I don't think it was ever stated, but growing up, I was made to believe that the Sunday morning worship experience was the most important aspect of my walk with Jesus—that if I missed a Sunday, I'd probably be struck by lightning. This was unintentional, for sure.

It's just too easy for church leadership to slip into this mindset. Every Sunday morning is coming, whether you like it or not. So significant energy has to go into making sure Sunday happens. From sermon preparation to ensuring our worship team is going to be ready, from making sure the gathering room is clean to being sure we have offering buckets in the right spot to cones in the parking lot, it all has to be ready for the collective gathering of a larger group of people.

And without the Sunday morning experience, you won't have an (gasp!) offering. So Sunday mornings have to happen. And they're unbelievably important to our faith.

Without relational connection, the church isn't the church. The church isn't a building to be occupied by people once a week. You don't believe that, and neither do I. The church is us, the people. We are the ones for whom Christ died. Not our buildings. Not our hymnals. Not our pews. It's the people who are the church. And without relational connection, you don't have a church.

At one level, my church experience growing up was good. I'm so thrilled that I grew up in a church that taught the gospel. My childhood church believed in the death, burial, and resurrection of Jesus. The people shared this message with others. But at another level, it didn't work. My growth as a disciple happened outside of the scope of the normal way of doing life in my local church. My experience left me with more knowledge, but at the end of the day, the church was just a show. Not something that I actively participated in, but something I observed. I was a soaker—a sponge, entering the doors ready to be filled with water, rather than simultaneously emptying my sponge *and* soaking it back up.

It was after my junior year of high school that my spiritual life began to rocket forward. Every Friday night, a group of us guys would get together to study the Scriptures, pray together, actively engage in conversations about Jesus, hold one another accountable for our growth, and top it off with late-night runs to Waffle House. And occasionally throw rolls of toilet paper on the neighbor's trees. Thankfully, I've grown since then. Kind of.

It was incredibly freeing and life-giving. At no other point in my spiritual life had my opinion been truly valued like with that group. At no other point had I been listened to rather than preached at. At no other point had I felt so closely connected relationally to people headed in the same direction as me. If it hadn't been for that small group, I would in no way be who I am today.

We were living out Acts 2:42-46: "All the believers devoted themselves to the apostles' teaching, and to fellowship, and to sharing in meals (including the Lord's Supper), and to prayer. A deep sense of awe came over them all, and the apostles performed many miraculous signs and wonders. And all the believers met together in one place and shared everything they had. They sold their property and possessions and shared the money with those in need. They worshiped together at the Temple each day, met in homes for the Lord's Supper, and shared their meals with great joy and generosity."

For me, church never felt like Acts 2:42-26. Never. It was when I lived this out in the context of healthy relationships that I grew and became a disciple. Spiritual growth is so much more than information transfer.

If your church views spiritual growth as a process that happens simply through watching a show, it may not be Jesus followers that you're creating. Without healthy relationships, you can't fully honor God. Let's look at some of the "one anothers" found in Scripture:

- Be devoted to one another. (Romans 12:10)
- Live in harmony with one another. (Romans 12:16)
- Love one another. (Romans 13:8)
- Be at peace with one another. (Mark 9:50)
- Wait for one another when you come together to eat. (1 Corinthians 11:33)
- Serve one another. (Galatians 5:13)

And it's really hard to do this in a corporate worship setting. It's really difficult to "be devoted" to someone else when you're looking at the back of their heads and listening to someone else talk. It's even more difficult to "serve one another" that way. Unless, of course, they need their hair brushed. Just the back part of it.

Without smaller communities, sitting in circles, not rows, it's nearly impossible to obey God in all things. Don't believe me? Then try this experiment. Read this verse, then I'll toss an activity your way. "Bear one another's burdens, and thereby fulfill the law of Christ." (Galatians 6:2)

Now, this coming Sunday morning, I want you to try to bear someone else's burdens. And if you have a small group that meets on Sunday morning, that doesn't count. Try to "bear one another's burdens" while your pastor is preaching. Or while you're walking in to the service. Or while you're singing. Or while you're filling up your cup of coffee. Even though my "burden" may be a second cup of coffee, I'm not sure that is what Paul had in mind when he wrote to the churches at Galatia.

In fact, Paul is talking about overcoming something. Maybe it's their sin. Maybe it's the sin of someone else. But sharing someone's burdens refers to helping walk someone back to the road of health and growth and grace. The burden of sin isn't one we're equipped to handle on our own. And to boil that down to "I'll pray for you" is to weaken this command. It would be like filling someone's coffee cup up with decaf. It takes the power right out of a good cup of coffee.

If you want to help people grow spiritually, get them doing life together. Not just getting together to watch a movie or hang out. Not just getting together to pray. Not just getting together to study the Bible. Not even just getting them together to serve. "Doing life together" encompasses so much more. How much more, you ask?

Let's walk through an exercise. Name 10 sermons you've heard in your life that have shaped you.

Sermon Title	Scripture References	Significant Takeaway

I doubt you could name ten. I can remember just a couple of sermons that impacted me in life-altering ways. In the moment, I walk out of so many sermons thinking, "Wow! That was amazing!" but then I don't apply the truth I've heard. Or I just simply forget it by the time my stomach growls for a Sunday afternoon lunch.

Now name 10 people that have invested in your life.

Name	How You're Different Because of Them

Much easier, wasn't it? It's easier because people are much more memorable than ideas. And people help us contextualize truth, rather than keeping truth at an intellectual arms-length. When we sit in an auditorium and listen to a preacher proclaim truth, it's easy to think, "I know someone who needs to hear this." Or, "That's a strong truth" without ever applying it.

Small groups are vital to the health of a local church. This reality is best understood when we put the why before the what. I love Sunday morning corporate worship. It energizes me to *worship* with other believers, and be challenged by good, solid preaching. But corporate gatherings alone will dry me up, spiritually. I need small group life. The times in my life when I was most alive spiritually have been the times when I was concurrently living life in honest, transparent community, not hiding behind a mask. Which is all-too-easy to do when you're in a corporate setting. Hiding is much tougher when you're living life with others.

1. *It's easy to hide in a large gathering.* It's tougher to hide in a small group. In fact, it's nearly impossible. Which, let's be honest, we'd prefer. Hiding is, at least in the short term, safer, easier, and a lot less messy. But for our spiritual growth, hiding is dangerous. And healing is found in confession with other like-minded believers.

2. *It's too easy to be passive during a sermon.* Sermons are primarily about soaking in information. It's a passive activity, for the most part. But we need to engage with the Scriptures while we engage with others. Good small groups don't allow the passive person to remain that way. Healthy small groups are more intentional about engagement.

3. *There is little to no accountability in corporate worship.* If you, in your heart, commit to some area of obedience during a sermon, who is going to help

you follow through with that? Our hearts are weak and our wills easily swayed, so we need others to walk alongside us. Follow-through is much easier in a small group than in a corporate setting, as we have people praying for our particular needs in smaller groups.

4. *We're prone to think we matter too little in corporate worship.* In a room full of people, we are tempted to think that, in the big scheme of things, we really don't matter. Unfortunately, we can fall into the trap of believing that our perspective, our gifts, our struggles, and our victories don't carry much weight. Small groups remind us that we are loved, cared for, and bring culture-shaping gifts to the table that God intends to use.

5. *We're prone to think we matter too much in corporate worship.* In a corporate setting, the other side of the coin is that we think our problems are the only ones that matter, that nobody really understands our struggles. Nobody could possibly know our pain. Nobody could remotely grasp our situation. Small groups remind us that others have problems like we do.

6. *We're prone to think, "They need to hear this" in corporate worship.* Don't lie. You've thought that. You've heard a sermon and said, "Oh man, I sure wish _____ was here. She needs to hear this." How arrogant are we when our only thought is how God

14

could be speaking to someone else, instead of to us directly? Small groups challenge us to apply Truth personally. Small groups don't let us get away with, "they need this."

7.) *We're prone to think, "This is only for me" in corporate worship.* When we're not thinking, "This is only for them," we can easily think, "This is only for me." We're good at making the world revolve around us, especially when it comes to feeling sorry for ourselves. Small groups keep us from cycling into destructive self-pity and loathing. They help us think rightly about ourselves and God, reminding us that we're only a part of the whole, and that other people are dealing with "life," too. We're told to "encourage one another daily" because our hearts are prone to being deceived by sin (Hebrews 3:13). We've got to have others to help us think rightly.

8.) *In a large gathering, when we cry, there's nobody to ask us, "What's going on?"* If you cry in a large gathering/worship service, it's easy for people to walk right by you, assuming someone else will stop and pray for you. But they don't know your story. They don't understand where the tears are coming from. They don't know what they'd say. They don't want to get too involved in your mess.

Small groups don't allow tears to go unchecked. If you cry in a small group, everybody notices. And everybody cares. Tears become everyone's problem, not just someone else's. If you're in pain, it becomes everyone's problem, because everyone's been praying for you, meeting with you, and growing with you. In other words, you have a relationship with them.

9. *No food is allowed in most worship gatherings.* There's a sign outside of the worship center in the church building where I'm on staff that says, "No food or drink allowed." Just because I "get it" doesn't mean I have to like it. Thankfully, we eat well in our small group, which I'm convinced is a God-honoring activity. I can't help but think of this key verse: "And day by day, attending the temple together and breaking bread in their homes, they received their food with glad and generous hearts" (Acts 2:46). Nothing helps a relationship form like a full belly.

10. *"Be quiet while the pastor is preaching!"* Small groups give you time to have deep, life-stirring conversations with people. Conversations that, if you tried to have them during a sermon in a worship service, people would look at you like you were crazy. They may even call security. And write blog posts about you.

Corporate worship services don't lend themselves to discussions that help with understanding and application. Small groups ask hard questions and allow for discovery. Learning isn't simply about transferring information. It's about interacting with that information. Learning involves poking and prodding and finding the holes, then overlaying it on your life to see where and how things need to change.

11.) *Convictions can go unchecked in corporate worship.* When the Spirit moves in small group, you've got time to slow down. But not so in a corporate worship service. When you're convicted in a room full of people, it's easy to slough it off, attributing it to the burrito you ate for dinner the night before.

In a small group, though, you have a chance to share those areas of your life that still need to grow. And you get to do it in a safe environment where people love you and have your best interests at heart. Then next week, they're going to ask you about it. Not because they have to. But because they want to because they care.

12.) *It's rare to pray for specific needs in a corporate worship setting.* Small groups pray for the specific needs of their group members. Not just generic, "God, thank you for what you're going to do here in this place" kind of prayers, but authentic pleading before God for others. Your needs are brought before God by others.

It's life-giving when you hear others praying for you. When you hear others begging God to show up in your life: where you work, in your home, and in your relationships. Have you ever heard someone verbally pray for you, specifically? If so, then you know what it's like to feel genuinely loved.

But small groups don't do everything well. Setting realistic expectations is important, so that we don't hope for something small groups can never give us.

One of the reasons that people get so frustrated with small group life is because they step in expecting something that small groups never promise to provide. Maybe they expect to get another sermon, like they did on Sunday morning. Maybe they expect to be constantly "fed." Maybe they expect to have to do no work. Maybe they want a "deep" Bible study. Maybe they want a seminary classroom-style experience.

Those qualities that a small group does well are summed in 1 Thessalonians 5:14: "And we urge you, brothers, warn those who are idle, encourage the timid, help the weak, be patient with everyone."

Using this verse, we can break down the important qualities of a healthy small group.

1. *"Brothers:"* Small groups help people "belong." It is absolutely essential in our walks with Christ that we

have brothers and sisters to whom we belong. This belonging is the foundation for the rest of the verse, and the foundation for living life in community as well.

We may prefer people to enter our churches who already believe, and have already begun to behave like good little Christians. But our culture today doesn't value believing and behaving first. Our culture values belonging before they believe. They want to know they're a part of something before they'll fully believe in it.

"Church" isn't merely a sermon factory. It isn't merely a place that cranks out information for us to download, increasing our knowledge about God. It's not just a place where church leaders tell people what to do and what not to do. It's an opportunity to help people experience what being loved really means, despite pain and confusion and the junk of life. It is a chance to show love to people who have never been truly loved. Church is a place to give grace to those who have never experienced it. It's a chance for us to worship God together, to pray together, and to serve together.

2. *"Warn those who are idle:"* We're not talking about an "idol." The word here is "idle." We are to speak truth and hope into the lives of people who are stuck. Who can forget that living life as a Jesus follower is one of action. One of serving and loving

and giving and going. Some of us need to quit planning and start doing.

Small groups are a breeding ground for personal ministry. When they're running efficiently, then everybody contributes. Everybody has a role. And everybody feels valued because of the contribution they're making.

Part of the responsibility of a small group leader is to help group members realize the work God's called them to, as well as their unique contribution in the Kingdom. (Ephesians 4:12) One way this is accomplished is through turning people loose to use their gifts, rather than hoarding all of the responsibility of ministry. We'll talk about this later, but for now, know that a vital responsibility of the group leader is not in doing everything necessary to help a group succeed. It's in sharing the responsibilities necessary (hosting, facilitating, communication, scheduling, researching curriculum, finding and meeting needs), and in so doing, equipping people to exercise their ministry muscles.

3. *"Encourage the timid:"* Fear is a reality for us in many different seasons of life. It grips our hearts and keeps us in bondage. Fear is one of the key reasons why we need other people. We need others to encourage us to take steps of faith. We need to know that others have our backs when we might fail.

Our journey of faith is too difficult to do on our own. Much too difficult. And yet, we sometimes push back on the very encouragement we need. Strange and twisted, no? Sometimes, I just want to give up. My body's tired and my mind is mush. I'd rather throw in the towel for the day. But when I press through, I find potential that I didn't know existed. "When you feel like you've used every ounce of energy you possess, you've still got extra reserve you can draw on," my coach once told me. Turns out he was right.

Encouragement communicates, "I believe in you," and everyone needs to hear it. They need to know that someone else sees the same vision they do. Someone else believes they can close that gap. Someone else believes they can produce more, and become the better version of themselves that God intended. Those you lead can't continue to do what God's called them to do without a timely word of encouragement. Genuine encouragement is a gift you can give daily. Turns out it's a biblical principle: "But encourage one another daily, as long as it is called 'Today,' so that none of you may be hardened by sin's deceitfulness" (Hebrews 3:13).

4. *"Help the weak:"* When small groups rally around people in their group, or others in their community, there's a deeper level of relationship than is found in most other areas of life. Helping the weak is something that healthy groups do well, especially

when we realize that we can use our pain to help others.

The church that decentralizes pastoral care is a healthy church. Instead of viewing care as something that has to be done by the paid staff, these churches empower members to take on significant responsibilities. Pastoral care is best when it's done by people who do life together, because there's a deep relationship involved.

5. "Be patient with everyone:" We're all at different points in our spiritual journeys. And at various points, each of us can be a difficult person. Whether we're walking through a mess ourselves, helping others deal with a mess, or trying to figure out what God's got next for us, we need others to be patient with us . . . and we need to learn to be patient with others. Just like God's patient with us. It's impossible to practice patience on your own. Being that we're all broken sinners, small groups give us a great chance to exercise patience with one another.

Notice one key component of all of these biblical commands: They involve being active. None of these commands can be accomplished while you're passive. None can be accomplished if you just look at group life as a sponge, expecting that following Jesus is about sitting around. If you go to a small group expecting to sit and soak, then you will dry up. If you go expecting to give deeply of yourself, then you will be filled.

This active nature of small groups is one of the most important reasons why small groups are critical to the health of every local church. Let me illustrate this point with a story. I played city-league basketball growing up. I wasn't that great. I was a scrawny white kid. But I was quick, and a decent shooter.

We played games on Saturday mornings at a local elementary school gymnasium. Overall, it wasn't a bad place to play. Plenty of seating. It was heated and cooled. And generally, it was clean. Generally.

Taking a look at the gym floor, you'd assume everything was fine. You could tell it had been used by decades of kids playing ball. The freshly veneered surface wasn't new, but it was acceptable. But there was a spot.

And if you were to take me to that gym today, I could close my eyes and walk to the spot. It was about 6 feet out from the basket on the side closest to the door. It was dead. Everybody playing knew the spot was there, but in the heat of a game, usually once or twice, the guy with the ball would forget about the spot, and go up for a layup with nothing in their hands. Running down the court at full speed, the ball that was once bouncing right back to the hand would bound no more, falling like a bowling ball to the gym floor and making the player look like a fool.

If only the maintenance crew had peeled back the hardwood and exposed the subfloor, it would've been a problem easily remedied. It wouldn't have cost a ton of money to fix the problem. But instead of fixing the underlying issue, maintenance decided to paint right over the spot and pretend it wasn't there. Just below the surface was this ugly hole, hidden by a freshly painted, freshly lacquered surface.

We do the same things spiritually, don't we? We put on beautiful masks to cover over a dark part of our story. We put a fresh coat of paint over the pain to tell the world we're perfectly fine. We slather on fresh lacquer and cover up something that we'd rather others not know is there.

We forget that God can repair and restore what's broken. We forget that God's in the *active* business of reconciling all things to Himself. And though that reconciliation might not look like we hope it will look, in time we'll grow to see the beauty. We'll experience God's love, forgiveness, and grace. We'll become new.

It's in this active process of restoring you and giving you hope that God will breath hope into someone else, too. But not if you paint over your issues.

Instead of healing, you'll cover over rotting wood. You will let the time bomb tick, while it's waiting to explode in the heat of battle. When you need the foundation of your life to hold the strongest, you'll find it crumbling as you live life in hiding.

You've got plenty of mess and pain and disappointments and frustrations. You have plenty of unmet expectations, unmet desires, and unreached potentials. So do I. Quit acting like you don't have problems. We're born without a mask. So let's quit putting a mask on. Be real and honest with someone. I'll start: I deal with insecurity. Not every day, but I have to battle against my flesh and remind myself that I'm loved by the King of Kings. I care too much what people think and what they say. "Sticks and stones may break my bones, but words can never hurt me" doesn't ring true with me. Names hurt. Words injure. And I battle with caring too much how others respond to my leadership.

Why small groups? Because this level of authenticity just doesn't happen in corporate gatherings. It takes intentionality and significant relationships. It takes meeting together regularly. It takes an *active*, not a *passive*, faith.

Get after it. Be active in a small group.

Questions:

What do you want your small group to look like? How many people? What will you study?

What will the goal of your small group be? Paint a picture of the person you want to produce.

Who will you invite to be a part of your small group? Have you prayed for them? If not, stop what you're doing. Put the book down. And go pray.

Chapter 3

No Failure to Launch

Philosophically, theologically, intellectually, and a lot of other words ending in "-lly," you're ready to launch! You're convinced that small groups are key to your spiritual growth. You're convinced that they're the key to your church's ongoing creation of disciples.

I've talked with so many people in this exact position. They know what they want. They're hungry for it. It's all they can think about. And it's moved beyond a theory for them. They're chomping at the bit!

Here is an example of a bit-chomper. It was the end of May, and "Randy" approached me about leading a small group. God had been working in his life. He had been in a healthy small group, and he was ready to launch out on his own and lead a new small group.

"That's great! Tell me about why you loved your last small group, Randy," I said. Randy elaborated on how God had worked in huge ways over the last six months through his small group. His marriage was in a better place than it had ever been. His personal relationship with Jesus was better than it had ever been. And he was ready to start a new small group.

"I'm pumped for you, Randy. So who are you going to invite? Who's going to be a part of your small group?" He looked at me like I'd just spoken those words in Latin. "I thought that was your job. To put people in my group."

So we talked strategy. And ministry.

"And what do you think about starting in August, when our whole church will be launching new groups? When summer vacations are over. Summer sports are done. And people are settling back into their normal routines? And when you can tap into the energy that our whole church will be creating?"

Strategy is unbelievably important.

It doesn't matter where you find your church organizationally. Whether you've got zero small groups. Or you're wanting to launch small groups alongside a Sunday school model. Or you're just trying to ratchet up the excellence level of your groups. This one idea may save you a lot of heartache, and help get the right players around the table.

It's called the test group.

Launch a Test Group

Everybody wants to be a part of something exclusive.

They want to be on the cutting edge. If Apple called you right now and said, "We're trying to figure out if this new product would work. Would you be willing to give it a shot?" You'd say yes with gusto. Don't lie. Even if you're not an Apple fan you would be curious. There's something compelling about trying something new for the purpose of helping others. Test groups help create early adopters. They give people an inside track to what's coming.

On the creator's side, test groups help an organization know what works and what doesn't. They allow an organization to try new things in new ways with new people, without the cost of a full product launch. Launching a new line of products drains a lot of resources, and it is incredibly risky. Test groups minimize the risk by helping determine— in advance—what will work and what will fail.

Test groups can work incredibly well in a local church, too. They're more strategic than simply starting with an idea, expecting that the whole church will instantly buy into it. They minimize risk and help get the right team to the table. And when you get them to the table, they can help shape the direction you're headed.

Let me define a test group for you.

Test group: A small group of high capacity, influential leaders who meet for a predetermined time for the purpose of exploring a new idea to implement. Let's break down the definition even further.

Small group: In this group, you're modeling what a healthy small group (according to your strategic mission and vision) looks like. The point isn't simply to cast an informational vision. It's to give people a picture of a healthy small group.

High capacity, influential leaders: Don't just recruit warm bodies. Recruit the people who are natural leaders. The people who, if they buy in to the idea of your small group, lots more will too. These people have natural leadership ability. They have followers. They may, or may not, be in significant leadership in your church. But you know they're leaders because wherever they go, others want to be around them.

For a predetermined time: The test group shouldn't last forever. After all, the goal is to equip these folks and turn them loose. Don't keep them here in your holding tank forever. Making your way through one or two rounds of curriculum should be adequate. Or, if you choose to not use curriculum, a couple of months should be long enough. Just make sure you end at a time where it's strategic to launch new groups, so that those in your test group can step right into group leadership.

For the purpose of exploring a new idea: Don't waste your time or their time. Be sure to model for your group what a healthy, authentic, vulnerable, and gospel-centered relationship looks like. These leaders will become the model for the rest of your church. They're the experts. Let them help you shape things, so that they're a dynamic part of the process instead of just your pawns.

Implement: Let them go! If you've got 4 couples in your group, then you should plan to launch four small groups. If you have five couples and a single person? Then launch six small groups. Use a 1:1 ratio. Or use a 2:1 ratio with co-leaders. Don't let these guys off the hook! They "get" the idea and strategy you're implementing better than anyone in the church. You need them to lead!

In launching a new initiative with groups, many times you cannot wait on the whole church. Don't just sit around and wait for there to be a church-wide initiative. You don't wait on your local church to tell you to read your Bible, do you? Or to pray? Or to share grace and hope with your co-worker? If God's laying it on your heart to start a small group, then there are some things we can do now.

Pray for potential group members. Call me old fashioned, but I think prayer still works. I believe the Bible when it says "I love the Lord because He hears and answers my prayers" (Psalm 116:1). Ask God to prepare their heart. Ask God to clear schedules. Beg God to put the right people into your group. Plead with God to form community quickly and beautifully with the people He brings together. Build up excitement now with the people you know. You may not be starting tomorrow, but you can get people excited about it now.

Start dropping hints. Begin telling people that you're going to start a new small group. And presume upon God's favor to do something huge in and through the group. Let them know that you'd be honored and excited for them to join once things get going. As you drop these hints, you also give them a chance to clear their schedules.

Start recruiting. Take the step beyond "hints." Recruit people to join, even before you launch. Get commitments from group members. Get commitments from a co-leader, too, someone who will help lead the group with you.

Pick out a handful of curriculum choices. Although you know a small group is much more than curriculum, potential group members want to know that there is some sort of plan and structure in place, that this group won't just be a dinner club, but will have a component of studying together involved.

Plan a start date. In the United States, the most strategic times to launch a group tend to be in the months of August and January. August works because many public school systems start during this month, and our culture tends to think "new" and "start" then. We also tend to think about resolutions for the year beginning in month of January as our calendar turns over. There are other times a group could start, but these tend to be the most strategic.

Recruiting

You can't launch anything without leaders. As John Maxwell says, "Everything rises and falls on leadership." Healthy small groups have healthy leaders.

One of the biggest challenges that churches face is in recruiting leaders. And I'm not talking about "warm bodies." Anybody can do that. If the requirement is "we'd prefer for you to be alive," then nearly everyone fits the bill, and your recruiting pool is like the Atlantic Ocean. But when you start adding requirements the pool shrinks considerably.

It's hard to overemphasize the importance of recruiting leaders. Get the right people, and small groups can soar. Get the wrong ones and you taint small groups for every member joining those groups. You'll be fighting an uphill battle moving forward, trying to convince people that their next experience will be better than the last.

Everywhere you go, look for leaders. There is no magic bullet when it comes to recruiting. I love

Robert Smith's approach in his book, *20,000 Days and Counting*. He tries to get 30 "NOs" every day. You've got to work through several "NOs" to get to the right "YES."

However, it's more than a simple numbers game. You can be strategic about how you ask people. Let's work through some ways to ask people strategically to serve.

1. Intentional apprenticing. Intentional apprenticing is a great way to recruit and deploy leaders. The beautiful part is that apprentices will have on-the-job training for months, and even years, before they're turned loose.

A small group apprentice is someone who is intentionally preparing for the day when he will lead his own group. She is participating in a small group now, helping with leadership, and being coached all along the way by a more seasoned small group leader. As long as you trust the leadership style, and spiritual maturity, of the group leader, then you can trust that the apprentice will start as a strong leader on her own.

The model can be a little slow at times, especially if you're in a church that's growing rapidly. You'll find yourself in a leadership deficit, having to wait 12-24 months for an apprentice to run their full cycle. If you want to speed it up a bit, do one of two things.

First, increase the number of apprentices in each group. Second, decrease the incubation time if you are comfortable with apprentices starting sooner.

2. Look to the end. Whenever a group is getting ready to end (our groups meet for 12-24 months), I sit down with the leader and ask for names of other potential leaders As people have done life together for a while, they've heard each other's stories, they've invested in each other, they've seen who may be cut out to lead a group. I've explained to them (through trainings, emails, personal conversations, etc.) what it takes to lead a group, and because they've built those relationships, they feel more comfortable recommending people for leading a group. You'll find the ground fertile for leadership at the winding down phase of a small group.

3. "There's not a group that works for me." Every time new groups start, I get this response. There's no group that meets during the 2.12 hours of free time they have in their life each week, that also meets in their neighborhood, and that is also studying what they want to study. All of the other groups meet too frequently. Or not frequently enough. And here's what I'll often say, "I'm so sorry. Would you like to start a new group? It can meet when and where you want it to meet."

For lots of people, "There's not a group for me" isn't

just an excuse. They're willing to take a step of faith, but every other night of the week is booked up for them.

4. In with the new. Start "new groups for new people." Launch a men's breakfast group. Start a "construction" group. Start a women's book club. Kick off a group that meets for Sunday lunch. Remember, if you've defined your win first, it's easier to step out and launch groups like this.

Starting these new types of groups is a way to get new leaders. It stretches and challenges people who think that they didn't fit in your system. It shows them that there is a place for them to lead with their gifts, passions, and talents.

5. Hit up the staff. There is a requirement at our church that staff members be in a group. But honestly, many of our staff members lead their group. Church staffers have influence with others. They're recruiting leaders for their ministry, or teaching from stage, or leading worship. And if they're leading a group, there's a good chance that they can fill it up without your help, and it will be filled with people who are bought into the character and reputation of that staff member.

If there are staff members not involved in small group life, then small groups aren't all that important to the life of your church. No matter how important you think they are, without a church leadership's involvement in group life, small groups will languish.

6. *Give me a break.* I give leaders the option (and make them feel no guilt or shame) to take a season off from leading a small group. Would I like for them to continue leading? Absolutely! Would it be easier on me if they continued leading! Absolutely! But in the long run, they'll end up frustrated and burned out because they've not ever had a break. Giving leaders a break may seem counterintuitive to getting new leaders, but I assure you: IT'S NOT! You're valuing the natural seasons of life when you give leaders a break from leading, and in that break, since they're not burned out, they become raving fans of small groups because most of the time, they begin to miss it. And though the break feels great, they're eager to get back in, so they start telling their friends.

7. *Gather 'round.* Know some folks that all want to meet on the same night? Maybe on the same side of town? Then your leader is at the table already! Here's what you can do: Get them in the same room, provide them some snacks, have them briefly share their faith story, talk about the value of group life, and tell them that you want to help them, this week, to find a leader. In fact, by then, you may have already spotted the leader.

Warning: This strategy is dangerous. You may get

someone who's absolutely unqualified and unequipped to be the leader. But Rick Warren once told me, "You can structure for control, or you can structure for growth, but you can't structure for both." And he's right. Do you believe that God is in control? Do you believe that God is the giver of gifts? Then He's the one who's given them that leadership ability.

You can train the other stuff. You can meet with them in a group or one-on-one, and help them grow spiritually. Leading a discussion, serving snacks, picking a curriculum, and hosting people are all trainable skills.

In this gather 'round meeting, I lay out the responsibilities of a group (in general), and ask for volunteers. I'll have people volunteer for each of these roles: Snack coordination, host, discussion facilitator, prayer request facilitator, service opportunities coordinator, and "fun" guy. Afterwards, I'll follow up with the discussion facilitator and walk through training with them.

I've seen a kind of revolution mentality develop in these settings. People come in, expecting to have a small group meeting, only to hear, "Sorry...you don't have a leader...but the leader is already here." A groundswell of excitement, we-can-do-this-thing mentality develops. And you've got a room full of people ready and willing to do something, and not just show up and soak up more knowledge. This strategy can be a powerful way to start a group, and a great way to find new leaders.

8. Line 'em up. Once, or twice, every year, start new short-term-focused small groups that lead out with studying the same thing. Most of the time, it makes sense to line up around a sermon series. Why does this ultra-focused, short-term small group experience help with recruiting leaders? First, it gives people a more manageable timetable for leading. It's a much easier sell, "You only have to lead for this group for four to six weeks."

You give people a chance to lead who would otherwise be too busy, who wouldn't commit to leading a group because they know next spring they're going to be locked down with their schedule. Short-term alignments give people the chance to lead when they can.

Second, you show your cards upfront. This way potential leaders know exactly what they're getting into when they sign up. They know that it's going to be based off the sermon on Sunday.

Third, these alignments lower the experiential leadership bar drastically, showing people that leading a group can be about simply inviting their neighbors, family, and friends into biblical community.

Come on! You can do this!

Questions:

Who could you ask to be a part of your test group? Write their names in the space below:

1. _____

2. _____

3. _____

4. _____

5. _____

When would be the most strategic time to launch a small group in your community? Is it worth waiting another few weeks, or a few months, to hit a peak time?

What do you think you'll study when you launch your group? Write out a few options below:

1. _____

2. _____

3. _____

4. _____

5. _____

What are you doing right now to prepare for your small group's kickoff?

If small groups are going to multiply, you have to recruit new leaders strategically. What strategies do you use to try to recruit new leaders? Which of the suggestions in this chapter could you use?

Chapter 4

Planning Connection

"Many will say they are loyal friends, but who can
find one who is truly reliable?"
Proverbs 20:6

The month after I started as a small groups pastor, I
was thrust right into a small group "launch." I'd been
on the job for less than a month, and I had to
assimilate a hundred people into new small groups.
Since we were a church plant, without a permanent
facility of our own, we decided to host an event at a
local hotel. We rented their ballroom out, set up
tables for group leaders, put out TVs with videos
explaining the value of small groups, and lifted
balloons because . . . hey, who doesn't like a good
helium balloon?

We invited people to show up that night and give us
45 minutes of their evening. In return, we promised
we'd help them find a small group. I was scared to
death. I didn't show it, of course. I was a pastor, so I
Jesus juked myself by quoting out-of-context verses.
I was scraping through every ounce of knowledge I
had, thinking through all of my seminary classes and
what they'd taught me. Seminary couldn't prepare
me for this night. But God did.

That night, we lived up to our promises. Kind of. We facilitated assimilation for a lot of folks, but there were a few things that bothered me. Ron Edmondson, my pastor at the time, wisely counseled me to write down everything I thought we should've done better. So I did.

1. Not everyone that came to the event got connected to a small group.

2. Not everyone who was interested in joining a small group even showed up at the event.

3. The event itself didn't help people who were more introverted. They clung to the walls.

I walked away from the event knowing that there were more people that couldn't make it to the event. We held it on a Tuesday night, and for some people, Tuesday nights would never work. Even though they wanted to attend, and join a small group, they couldn't because of their schedules. Our system prevented them from joining.

On top of that, there were some people who came, but still didn't get into a group. They didn't find the group that worked for them. Whether that was because they were distracted by the kids they brought to the event, a potential group was too far from their house, or they thought that they could join a potential group later, they didn't join.

Throughout the event, I noticed lots of wallflowers. People who were uncomfortable in crowds. The event felt like speed dating to them, moving from table to table and interviewing potential group leaders like you'd interview a potential date.

The next day, after the event was complete, I realized something. The work of assimilation wasn't over, but had just begun. We now had to assimilate people together to form the group. It's one thing to get people to sign up for a group, and make a half-hearted commitment to showing up. It's quite another to bind people together in healthy, biblical community.

If you want to get people plugged in to small groups, there are two steps you have to take:

1. Helping people find a group and physically connecting them with others.

2. Ensuring they have a stellar group experience—spiritually, emotionally, and experientially connecting them with others (more on this experience in chapter 5).

The Best Way is Always Through Trusting Relationships

Before we get into the specifics of different types of small groups launches, let's get one thing out of the way. The best way to form a small group is purely through relationships. Not an event the church puts on. Not through an online sign up. Not through a church-wide initiative. It's through relationships.

When you have a prior relationship with someone, there's a trust that's already been built. You've laid the groundwork that typically takes months to do in a small group. So much of a small group's success or failure is contingent upon trust. Trusting what's said in the group stays in the group. Trusting what you say comes from a heart of love. Trusting that small group is a safe place for me to be transparent and not to be ridiculed. Trusting that God's going to use this time in my life.

When you've already built trust with someone, there's less risk for them, and a higher potential that they'll stick in your group. There's no wondering if they can trust you or not. Trust is earned, and small groups can do tangible things to build this trust.

Make the Connection with an Event

One-on-one invitations and relationships work best for connecting people to small groups. However, it's not the only way to make a connection. The most effective way I've found to connect people in small groups, when it's not through relationships, is through "the event." Call it whatever you want: Connect Now, Group Link, Group Up, Connections, or something else entirely. The event is a chance for you to launch multiple small groups at the same time by inviting people to a neutral location (not someone's home) up to four times a year. At this event, people will meet group leaders and commit to a new small group.

I've hosted this event on Sunday mornings, immediately following the worship service. But this event can be done on Sunday nights, inviting people to come back to the church building, or on Wednesday nights, inviting people to come back to the church building when they drop their students off for services. I've heard of churches doing these in conjunction with a cookout, a block party, or a family night.

The major decision for a small group event involves the choice of a day—Sunday morning or some other time. Both have their advantages and disadvantages.

Sunday morning: This day is the time when you will have the highest participation, because you're making it as easy as possible for people to take the step to join a group. All they have to do is fill out a card and drop it in the offering bucket. When you combine sign-up-Sunday with a message speaking to the importance of living life in community with others, you're lining up the small group stars.

With a Sunday morning event, you'll also have the highest drop-out rate. Your numbers will be high for people interested in joining a group, but the commitment rate will be low. People are excited about joining on a Sunday morning. But when Tuesday night happens, and their only point of contact for their new group is that they met a leader for 5 minutes this past Sunday morning, the likelihood of them actually showing up decreases drastically.

A time other than Sunday morning: There are lots of options under the "any other time" category. But in the end, they are similar in one way: You don't get nearly as many people interested. But those that do come will be committed. The ones that show up for your event will sink their teeth in and join a group. Your retention rate from that event will be massively higher than if you'd done the event on Sunday morning. You won't have groups starting with 20 in attendance and by week two have an attendance of 5. You'll be starting groups with 10 in attendance and retaining those 10!

Alternatives to Having an Event

If holding a small groups event is not a good option

for your church, other strategies exist.

Alignment campaigns. This church-wide initiative was mentioned in chapter 3 as a way to find new leaders. But it's also a way to assimilate people into small groups. And it's quite effective. In an alignment, all of your current small groups will study the same curriculum for a short season, usually the duration of a sermon series. In addition, you'll work to form new small groups that will use this same curriculum as their launching point.

This campaign gives every single person in your church the chance to start a small group. You're providing the curriculum. You're providing the content (from your Sunday morning series). You're providing the training (leading up to their small group launch). They're providing the location (their home, work, or anywhere they can carve out time each week) and the people (their friends, neighbors, and co-workers).

You have the potential to launch as many small groups using this method as there are families in your church. Because everyone knows someone else they could invite into their home to study the Scriptures and grow spiritually. You might be shocked by how many people would say, "No" to an invitation to worship with you on Sunday morning but will say, "Yes" to coming into your home to talk about God.

The first step is to choose something accessible. Don't just pick any sermon series on which to align your church. Choose one that is shorter (4-6 weeks is ideal) and easy (for people outside of the faith) to engage with, and that's stimulating. Topics that are less than ideal include:

- The travels of David
- The history of Nehemiah
- Temple archaeology
- 42 weeks through the book of Esther

Pick topics unbelievers will find interesting:

- Marriage
- Your Life Purpose
- Understanding the Bible
- Building Healthy Relationships
- Love

Make it both accessible to unbelievers and accessible to your church culture. Just make sure you choose topics that make it easy for church members to invite their friends to study.

The curriculum. You can write it yourself. Or you could hire someone to write it for you. There are companies that do just this for a small fee. Just be sure to let them know who you're targeting through your study. They're typically really flexible.

Don't leave me hanging. As the series comes to a close, be sure to follow up with the new group leaders, helping them to transition to full-time small groups if they're interested. Link them up with a coach. Provide further training and care. Help them find their next curriculum to study. And help them stay together as a fledgling group.

Just Do It

Some churches take advantage of this. There's no real "strategy." The only drive is connecting people. Anytime. All of the time. The thought process works like this:

- Small groups are our primary method of creating disciples.
- People need small groups.
- We have small groups.
- Why wait?

This is done through a variety of methods. It could be an announcement to fill out cards, which will be divvied up into appropriate groups. It could be a small groups "book" that describes where each group meets, and how to contact the leader. It could be a setup in the hallway with information on each group. Or something similar posted online.

Though it may appear haphazard on the surface, this method can work. It can be a solid way to connect people to groups. I prefer implementing a strategy alongside the "just connect people." The longer a group meets, the more difficult it becomes to connect new people. A group solidifies themselves within 6-8 weeks, and while adding people is possible, it becomes increasingly difficult. It's easier to launch new groups than to add to old ones. That way everyone can start off on the same page.

But don't just think you can tell people about small groups once, and they'll begin to flock like the salmon of Capistrano. You've got to work to get people excited about connecting, investing, and taking steps of faith together.

Building Anticipation

I love being a dad. It's not easy, by any stretch of the imagination. But it's good. And one thing that we as a family love is laughing together. And one way I personally promote that is by tickling my son. It makes both of us laugh hysterically. I don't know if you've ever tickled a 2-year old, but it's pretty funny. It's hard not to laugh along with them. And I noticed this the other day: my son starts laughing before I even tickle him.

I just curl up my hand, like I'm going to tickle him and just get it close to his belly, and he starts to cringe up in laughter. It's not one of those courtesy, half-hearted chuckles we adults give to make someone feel okay about a flopped joke. It's an all-body laughter. And the anticipation plays into his overall tickle experience.

It's healthy to build anticipation in launching small groups, too. Asking people to wait until launch day to join a new group isn't such a bad thing. It helps build anticipation and excitement, building the tension of need in their heart.

If you have an equal opportunity to join a group every week, then there's no impetus to join now. There is no reason to join next week if I can join in a month. And we'd like to think that life will get less busy in a month. But it never does. If you believe that the message you're presenting is valuable, why would you not create tension and anticipation for what's coming next? TV shows do it. Movies do it. Radio talk shows create it. Teachers create it. Guys who want a second date build it. Build the anticipation, and leave people begging for what's coming.

The How of Building Anticipation

The how of building anticipation is not as difficult as you might think. There is a convergence of leadership, stories, and marketing. Let me explain.

The most influential person in the room. Who's the most influential person in the room? The one with the mic. Your pastor is the mouthpiece for small groups. If your pastor preaches about the value of group life, uses illustrations from his own small group experience, and week after week drives home the importance of living life in community with others, then the congregation will follow suit.

If your pastor lives life as if authentic community is just for others, then those others will think the same thing. If your pastor is too busy to join a small group, your congregation will be too busy, too. If small groups are perceived to be a waste of time for your pastor, the same perception will permeate your church. Your pastor has to live it. And talk about it. Publicly.

Tell stories. Telling stories motivates people. The power of a good story can influence people in a tangible way. If you highlight people's experiences of life change and growth, rather than just declare edicts from the pulpit, you will motivate people's hearts. Edicts tell you what you have to do, but stories come from people who love their small groups. Whether you shoot short videos highlighting stories, bring people on stage, share them on Facebook, or have your pastor share them as illustrations during the sermon, gathering and sharing stories is the most effective way you can help people buy into group life.

Marketing strategy. Anticipation is built on the heels of waiting for something good to come. Anticipation isn't found in immediate gratification. Asking people to wait a few weeks, or even a month or more, to join a small group, isn't always a bad thing. Especially if what you're offering is going to be really, really good.

"I'm sorry, we don't have a group for you to join right now. We're launching new ones in 3 weeks. If you can wait just a little bit, we're putting something together that's going to be amazing. You're going to love it!"

See what I did there? In asking you to wait, I got you excited about what's coming. I've begun to make a raving fan out of you before you've even joined a group. Will you lose a few people in the process of asking them to wait, not connecting them right now? Probably. But the people you gain because you're starting new groups instead of forming one through piecemeal over time will far outweigh the negative consequences of losing a few marginally invested people.

You're offering a better experience by having them wait. Believe it. We've talked about the most strategic times to launch small groups: August and January. In between those times, consider something smaller scale to connect new folks.

And as much as you can, try to clear your church calendar on the day you launch new groups. Other important things will vie for the attention of your church. But if you believe that life change happens best in the context of intentional relationships (small groups), and you only have a few strategic times each year where it's optimal to join a group, then work hard to bump other announcements and launches to different Sunday mornings.

Christian Fatigue Syndrome

Growing up, I went to church a lot. On any given week, we had Sunday morning services, Sunday school, youth choir, discipleship classes, student ministry, Tuesday night outreach, Bible drill, Royal Ambassadors, and Friday night at the gym. Sprinkle in the occasional Saturday brunch, outreach event, and Judgment House, and our lives revolved around being at the church building. I was blessed with committed parents who set me on a trajectory that would shape my life in incredible ways.

I remember vividly one late Sunday afternoon sitting on the back deck grilling with my dad. My little brother was swimming in our blue kiddie pool, and mom was there taking it all in. I felt guilty the moment this thought passed through my head, but I let it pass anyway. I guess I was just a little devil child. It was a fleeting thought: "I sure wish we could just skip out on going to church tonight."

As I thought it, fire from heaven spit down into my eyes and scorched me. Turns out, though, the rest of my family was thinking the same thing. We weren't trying to be heathens, choosing to indulge in our sin rather than worship Jesus. We just all wanted to be together as a family and relax (Sabbath) instead of cleaning up, putting on our "Sunday best," and driving across town to our second worship service of the day.

Maybe you grew up in that sort of environment too. It's not that churches set out to heap burdens on people and create guilty feelings when they even think about not attending a Sunday evening service. "Stuff" just happens. One good idea gets thrown on top of another, and before you know it, every night of the week is loaded with a different event.

No church drifts into simplicity. Currents take a church towards complexity. Since each of these events is linked with a grand idea, a dynamic leader, and the heart of a person who wants to lead people to Jesus, they're incredibly difficult to stop even when the timing is right. "Simple" churches give families the time to invest in one another. Time to serve their community. Time to enjoy a Sunday Sabbath. Time to minister to their neighbors. Time to invite people into their home. Time to be the church, rather than simply go to church.

Complex churches give people "Christian Fatigue

Syndrome," wearing people out with good things and not freeing them up to do what's best. When people are hit with CFS, they become desensitized to authentic worship, heartfelt evangelism, and authentic community. Small groups are not just another church activity to put on busy calendars. Small groups are the heart of authentic community.

Questions:

What do you think would work best for you and your church as far as launching groups? "The Event" or something else?

If the best way to launch a small group is through relationships, what are you doing right now to prepare for that?

What is the best vehicle to share stories in your church? How are you going to get stories of life change in small groups in front of your church?

How do you feel about asking someone to wait for a small groups launch, rather than joining a group right now? How might this play into their overall anticipation of small groups?

Is your lead pastor bought into the mission and vision of your small groups?

Chapter 5

Keeping a Good Thing Going

"The end of all things is at hand; therefore be self-controlled and sober-minded for the sake of your prayers. Above all, keep loving one another earnestly, since love covers a multitude of sins. Show hospitality to one another without grumbling. As each has received a gift, use it to serve one another, as good stewards of God's varied grace: whoever speaks, as one who speaks oracles of God; whoever serves, as one who serves by the strength that God supplies—in order that in everything God may be glorified through Jesus Christ. To him belong glory and dominion forever and ever. Amen."
1 Peter 4:7-11

A well-oiled machine still needs regular oil. If you want your small groups to be well-oiled machines, you've got to do some work.

"Hey Ben, welcome! We're so glad you're here! You'll love it at our church. We love our pastors and we love our small group! Oh yeah, and we've been leading a group now for about a year, and really need some help. We've hit a snag, and have no idea what to do. Can you give us a call sometime today? Thanks!"

That was the call I got on Tuesday morning, the first week I was on the job as a small groups pastor. I was absolutely terrified to call them back. Terrified that I'd have nothing to say. Or, worse yet, that I say something wrong, and tank a good small group. I didn't want to be seen as a fraud, knowing nothing about which I was hired to do.

But I had no idea how to respond. No advice to give. No "I've seen it this way, so . . . " No perfect Bible verse to wow them. I could get small groups started. But keeping them going? Nope. That was beyond my pay grade.

Maybe you're in the same boat I was. You understand how to get groups going. You know how to operate in a healthy small group. You know what the finished product looks like for a small group, but you don't' know how to sustain that health over time. You don't know how to structure a small group to take steps of faith.

Can I share something with you? There is no magic bullet. No secret pill you can give group leaders. No one-stop-shop for your small group health needs.

The "Late" Test

When a group leader launches a new small group, they're curious. They want to know if they're going to have a successful group. They don't know if their group is going to stick, if people will come back, or if they'll take steps of faith together.

How do you know if your new small group is going to "work"? How do you know if they're going to stick together and grow and have dynamic stories of life change? Is it that you have solid biblical discussions right off the bat? Is it that for the first few weeks everybody shows up? Is it that they've already started talking about the group serving together? Is it just that sense of "peace," that fluffy feeling in your stomach you sometimes get?

I submit something different. I saw the #1 marker of success in the small group that my wife and I lead, and I saw it last night. How do I know we're going to have a successful group? They stayed at our house until almost 11:00. And we started at 6:30.

Relationally, we've already made deep connections. When we say, "Amen," we're not done. Our group isn't defined by our study alone. Our group isn't defined by the fact that we meet on Tuesday nights. Our group isn't defined by our life stage or our kids' ages. Our group is defined by significant relationships, built around the stories God has written with our lives and the story He's writing with us together as a group.

We've built authentic community quickly. It just took us a few weeks, but God's woven us together beautifully. We've made a priority out of getting to know each other at a level deeper than the surface. And it's working. Late into the night every Tuesday night. If your group hangs around after you say, "Amen," you're doing something right. Without significant relationships, your group won't last. Mark my word. But how do you sustain something like this over time? Let's explore that question.

The Rhythm of a Small Group

I am a runner. And I've got to be one of a handful of people who truly loves it. I love the smells. I love the breeze. I love the sweat. I love not being able to hear my cell phone ring. And I love the feeling when I'm done. Unless I get off pace. When my rhythm is off, I don't enjoy it nearly as much.

If I run faster than my normal pace, I find myself gasping for air the whole run. I also find myself hating running. I think, "Why am I outside doing this? I could be doing something—anything—else. I'll never do this again." Seriously, in one off-paced run, I'll question the whole fabric of my love of jogging.

If I run slower than my normal pace, I find myself bored. I think, "Why am I outside doing this? I'm just wasting my time. I could just be walking. At least then I wouldn't be sweating so much." Get me off of my pace, and running isn't fun anymore. Though my rhythm took a while to create, I know it when I'm off-base. I know it instantly.

Just as rhythms in running are important, so are rhythms in other areas of life. We need our rhythms at work, knowing when to show up, when to take a break, and when to hit the gas. We need rhythms in our physical life. Rhythms that help us rest, engage, eat, work out, and grow. We need rhythms in our spiritual life, cycling between solitude, community, corporate worship, and private disciplines.

If rhythms are so important throughout our lives, why would we think they'd be a non-issue in group life? As John Ortberg says, "Spiritual transformation cannot be orchestrated or controlled, but neither is it a random venture. We need some kind of support or structure, much as a young vine needs a trellis. We need sails to help us catch the winds of the Spirit. All of us know the frustration of random, haphazard efforts that lead nowhere in spiritual life. We need a plan for transformation."

So the regular rhythm that my small group employs is this:

- Gather weekly. Each week, gather for fellowship, Bible study, prayer, and food.
- Party monthly. Once/month, gather together to celebrate the work God's doing in your group.

- Serve quarterly. Once/quarter, get out of the walls of your group, and serve your community.

Gather Weekly

Is gathering that important? Traditional thinking in American Protestant culture values individual time with God. We purport that as the center of spiritual growth. Go in your room, shut the door, and study.

Master the art of the "quiet time." Just you and God. Read a book by yourself. Put headphones on and listen to a podcast by yourself. Go sit on a hammock and pray by yourself.

This mentality bleeds into our worship services too. We sit in a classroom-style setting, with rows of chairs in a Sunday school class or a worship center. One person, the teacher or preacher, proclaims the Truth we need to digest, while being certain to keep our hands to ourselves. There's no talking allowed in either setting. I even remember a note in the bulletin of a local church I attended saying, "If you have to get up during worship, please do so before the sermon starts in order to not distract the work of the Holy Spirit." I believe some think the Holy Spirit throws up His hands in utter what-am-I-going-to-do-now fashion as soon as a kid gets up to go to the bathroom.

Contrast this practice with traditional Jewish styles of learning. Jews seldom study Torah alone. The study of Torah is a social and communal activity. Most commonly, Jews study Jewish texts in pairs, a method known as *havruta* ("fellowship"). In *havruta*, the pair struggles to understand the meaning of each passage and discusses how to apply it to the larger issues addressed and even to their own lives.

Studying, wrestling, and seeking hard after God is done communally. We Protestants have missed that. With our rows of people, quiet services, quiet times with God, and personal spiritual growth plans, we inadvertently push people towards an individualistic faith.

My friend, James Grogan, says, "Circles are better than rows." He may have stolen that phrase, but since I don't know who said it first, I'll give James the credit. Circles promote group growth, unity, and a combined synergy towards knowing God, encouraging each other, correcting each other, and pushing each other towards God's best. The reality is that I don't know everything there is to know about the Bible. God hasn't revealed all angles and varied beauty of truth to me. Your life experiences have given you a certain interpretation of the texts of Scripture that help to know God more fully. Your upbringing, your failures, your pain, your victories, your passions, they all help people know God better. Not that if we study and engage God together that we have to walk out of that clones of one another. I'm still me and you're still you. But our collective relationships with our Creator are multiplied together.

Gather together and studying God's Word has several <u>advantages:</u>

1. We both work to fulfill the Great Commission. Iron sharpens iron, and together we push one another to love Jesus more.

2. We build fellowship. The early church followers devoted themselves to fellowship, and God honored them in this practice. You shouldn't walk alone in your faith.

3. We fight against pride, realizing we're not the only ones with the "right" answer. On your own, you're prone to thinking you've got the best insight, the most understanding, and all of the "right" answers. If you thought you didn't, you'd change your mind, right?

4. Past experiences are (at least) doubled, adding new flavors and angles to the truth. You only have one past, one set of experiences, and one mind. And thus only one insight into the vast depth of Scripture.

5. We can laugh together. And that's vital for our growth. If you laugh on your own, while it's just you and God talking, then it can get a little weird.

6. We don't get stuck on questions. We're less prone to getting stuck, because we can help each other out of our ruts of questions.

7. There's built-in accountability. I can't short-cut the process of learning if I'm constantly being pushed and challenged by someone else. Alone, in a large room, though, it's easy to disappear, not process, and not challenge myself.

8. You're prone to being narrow-minded by yourself. We can so easily dive straight into narrow-minded legalism and bigotry when we make our faith only about ourselves.

9. You only have two ears to hear from God, alone. When you read the Scriptures and study them alone, you're limited to your own ears. God speaks to other people besides you.

10. A cord of three strands is not quickly broken (Ecclesiastes 4:12). Obeying God is too hard. Trying to understand, and obey, the Scriptures will break you. If you go it alone. Some of us Protestants have missed the boat

when we study, prepare, and examine the Scriptures by ourselves. We're better together.

The Thing about Food

If you want your group to fail more quickly than any other way, don't offer food. Seriously, just start your Bible study the moment your group time starts. Then close in prayer and ask people to go home. Then watch your group never get off of the ground.

Ice cold soda and desserts can help any group. During the first few group meetings, people are nervous, they don't know others, don't know what to expect, and aren't fully comfortable striking up (and maintaining) a conversation with someone. Meals give you a natural reason to congregate together. You're sitting around a table together, or around the living room together, for a specific purpose: to eat. There's just something psychologically important about eating together.

When you serve snacks and you're not the only one who brings them, you share the responsibility for making sure your group succeeds, giving one more person a chance to contribute to the group. Which means that if you're there, and they're there, you've got at least a small group of two every week.

Also, depending on the time that your group will

meet, offering a meal as part of your group overcomes one more excuse people may give for not coming. If your group is at 6:30 on a weeknight, and someone gets off work at 5:00, home by 5:30, and then has to take the kids to the babysitter, and has to eat before they go to group, often they'll just choose to eat a slower dinner in favor of group. If a group member skips group a couple of times for dinner, you can just about guarantee she is not coming back. But if she knows that a meal will be served, she is more likely to show up.

Meals help reorient our thinking, too. Tim Chester in *Meals with Jesus* says, "Meals slow things down. Some of us don't like that. We like to get things done. But meals force you to be people oriented instead of task oriented. Sharing a meal is not the only way to build relationships, but it is number one on the list." If you want your group to succeed, plan to eat together. It doesn't matter what your group decides: snacks, a meal, or dessert. But decide on something.

The Thing about Hosting

If a group is going to be sustained over time, you've got to do hosting right. There is nothing in the Bible (directly) that would tell me how I should host a small group in my home. But there are truths I've found, and tested, that will work for you, too, if you'll give them a shot.

Leave the pile of mail. My wife and I were doing the busy-bee clean of our house one Tuesday late afternoon before small group showed up. We had about 45 minutes before the first couple would knock on the door, so we were feverishly dusting, scrubbing, and straightening. When the busy-bee nightmare happened: someone knocked on the door. I looked at my wife, and our faces dropped, hoping it was just the UPS guy dropping off a package and bolting back to his brown truck. I unlocked the door, trying to get a peek through the crack as I opened so I could prepare my heart.

"Oh, hey guys! You're early!" I said to the group members, who were beaming. "Oh, we are? We thought we were 15 minutes late. When does group start?"

They were early, and my heart sank as I realized we were nowhere near ready. I watched as their eyes scanned the room, realizing they were quite a bit early. It was embarrassing for me. "We're glad you're here, but you're going to have to excuse the mess. We're not quite done cleaning yet. Don't mind that dust bunny. Or the pile of mail. Or the cups in the sink."

Their response changed our relationship, and changed the way I thought about cleanliness for small group. "Don't mind it? We'll get this thing knocked out. Give me the vacuum cleaner. Honey, you go sweep the front porch." And for the next 45 minutes, they helped us get things ready. And then they dropped this bomb: "We're just glad to know we're not the only ones whose house isn't perfect all of the time." Isn't it a relief when you see someone else's house that isn't perfect? It's like a reminder that you're in the clear, especially when that house is your pastor's place.

This story is a picture of the kind of vulnerability that's necessary to "do life together" with people. If your house is perfectly neat and tidy each and every time, you communicate that your life is perfectly neat and tidy all of the time. That there are no dust bunnies in your life. No piles of unchecked mail. No weed left un-pulled. Through your perfect facade, you give the air of a perfect marriage with perfect children, of a life with a perfect job and a perfect life of holiness. And that's dangerous ground to stand on.

So my challenge to you is to clean your house, but don't sweat it. Invite people into your life. If you've always got a pile of mail on the entry way table, then leave it there. Don't feel like everything has to be perfect. Through this, you'll communicate boatloads of hope—that people can come as they are to small group. They can be who they are, warts and all. They can bring their victories, and also their struggles. The pile of mail tells them that it's okay to not have everything completely put together all of the time, and that this is a safe place to be real.

Su Casa, Mi Casa. If you follow the "leave the pile of mail" rule, you'll have a better chance of following the "Su Casa, Mi Casa" rule, too. Rotating homes is a skill that the best small groups have developed. It helps everyone feel like they're a part of the group, and that they have something to contribute. They will feel more invested in the group, even as they go through the routine of cleaning and straightening their home in preparation for the group to arrive.

If you have ever hosted a small group in your home, you know that it can be a bit vulnerable. You're inviting people into the place where you live. No more pretense. No more hiding. You're pulling back the curtain. Especially if they follow the "leave the pile of mail" rule. It also gives them a chance to not have to travel to their small group that night. I know this sounds minor, but we've found it's a great way to help get people connected in a group that doesn't meet in their same neighborhood. "This group doesn't meet right beside you? No worries. You can be one of the group hosts, and some months you won't have to travel at all!"

A small group isn't just one person leading others. A small group has a "we're in this together" mentality, and this is beautifully seen as a group rotates hosting responsibilities.

The Thing about Prayer

"This is your house. You've got the floor to pray if you want," I whispered to my friend as we gathered together in his kitchen, people spilling into the dining room prior to small group. Lots of people showed up that night, eager to engage, catch up on the week, and dig into the homemade meatball subs simmering on the stove top. Facial expressions speak much louder than words. Unless, of course, you are screaming into a megaphone, in which case those words speak louder than your facial expressions. But in most instances in life, knee-jerk facial expressions speak what's on your heart loudly. In this moment, I knew I'd inadvertently put my friend in an awkward spot.

"Umm. Ok. Let's do this" he whispered back, shrugging his shoulders to shake off that nervous feeling of inadequacy and I-have-no-idea-what-I'm-doing. He positioned himself so that the full group could see and hear him, and began to tie the laces of the new "spiritual leader" shoes he was taking for a spin around the block. "Well, guys, welcome to our home," he squeezed through a forced smile. "We're glad you're here," he said as he communicated genuineness, making eye contact with everyone looking up. "I've never done this before. Well, out loud, anyway. But let's pray."

He prayed the most simple, God-honoring, easy-going, authentic prayer I may have ever heard.

There was nothing profound about his prayer. Nothing particularly to note from an outsider's perspective. But knowing the internal battle of his heart, combined with the fact that he'd never taken the spiritual lead publicly like this before, it was beautiful. I believe this step of faith he took into unknown (for him) territory has set his family on a pathway to spiritual growth like he's never known. Though the prayer may not have sounded radical to you, it was a risky, wall-shattering step towards Jesus.

It was our small group that got him ready for this. And I know how we did it. There is a way to structure prayer time that encourages prayer. And there is a way to structure prayer time that encourages people to think you're amazing and eloquent. One way honors God. One way honors you and your flowery vocabulary.

The more you use theologically technical, complicated words when you pray out loud, the more you'll encourage people to shut down during prayer time. Why? Because they don't have that vocabulary. At some level, praying out loud is like public speaking. Glossophobia (fear of public speaking) strikes 75% of people at some level, and we as a culture are deathly afraid of speaking in public. Maybe it's a twisted form of pride that we need to work through, but speaking publicly strikes a fear into most people's heart. Combine that with the fact that people don't know the words you're using, they're afraid to appear "immature" spiritually in front of other people. They don't know what to say, and it's easy to shut people down during group prayer time through the words you use.

You, the leader, can lead group members to take radical steps of faith by the way you pray out loud. Pray simply. Pray as if you're talking to a friend. God is not impressed by your theologically charged language. He wants your heart, not your words. In fact, when you use words that don't encourage others to unite with you in prayer, you sound a lot like the hypocrite from Matthew 6. You've gotten your reward already, and the reward isn't that God heard you.

Do you want to encourage others to begin praying? Pray simply. Use normal language. And keep your prayers short. Pray for a specific request, thank God that He showed up, and move on. It's in that process of simplicity that group members begin to think, "This prayer thing . . . it's not so hard. Maybe I can try talking to God, too." Last time I checked, talking to God for the first time is a radical, beautiful step of faith.

Party Monthly

I just want to take a minute to say that we're all proud of the way you've done your research and found the most biblical curriculum. Your small group has an airtight, foolproof theology. You can move from a discussion on the Nephilim to ecclesiology, then weave in a bit of distinction between Calvinism, the resurrection, and eschatology. You can facilitate a discussion, minister to the EGRs (Extra Grace Required), fill the empty chair, raise up apprentice leaders, and plant new groups. Your group is even "missional," consistently serving your neighborhood and community. Group members are working to baptize and make disciples of all nations, starting with their families and neighbors.

But one thing is missing. Your group isn't fun. Sometimes it's boring, actually. Sometimes people only come because they feel like they are supposed to. So here's my plea to you: incorporate fun, life, and humor into the life of your group.

Why would you focus on fun? Here are six key reasons:

1. If it's not fun, people won't come back. It's possible to get more information in a more convenient time in a more convenient way through many other means. Podcasts, books, blogs, and forums offer information and

discussion environments at any time of the day, every day of the year. What separates small groups from each of these environments is the relationship, face-to-face aspect. Make sure you maximize this!

2. If there's no fun, it's life-sucking. If your group is intensely serious, it can drain the life right out of people. We're only wired to take so much seriousness. And often, every other environment in our lives gives us plenty of seriousness.

3. If there's no laughter, people are missing out on great medicine. "A joyful heart is good medicine, but a crushed spirit dries up the bones" (Proverbs 17:22). Maybe what hurting people need isn't more medicine, but a healthy small group. They need to laugh together so hard that they snort. They need to laugh at themselves. They need to laugh at a corny joke. I'm not sure how it works, but after a difficult day at work—with the kids, with finances, with in-laws—laughing helps to melt away stress and anxiety, bringing healing to your aching bones.

4. Have you ever belly-laughed? Seriously, there is not much that is more redemptive than belly-laughing with someone in your small group. If you've laughed that way, from your

gut, you know what I mean. Laughing so hard you embarrass yourself. Laughing so hard you even forgot what you were originally laughing about, and other people join you not because what was said was funny but simply because you're laughing so hard.

5. When we have fun together, we show others that we serve a good God. Check this out: "Then our mouth was filled with laughter, and our tongue with shouts of joy; then they said among the nations, 'The Lord has done great things for them'" (Psalm 126:2). Did you catch that? When our mouths are filled with laughter, others are convinced that God has done great things among us. Could the flip-side be true? If our mouths aren't filled with laughter, could people become convinced that the God we serve isn't good? That he doesn't take delight in loving His people? That the God we give witness to is ultimately boring, and the eternity with him that we say will be wonderful is painted as dull and lifeless?

6. Laughter builds community. Laughing together can help your group bond in a rich way quickly. Don't neglect times of fun and laughing. Relish those times together. Jokes that carry from week to week, laughing at random things, and having fun together help set the stage for

deep discussions, building trust among those in your group.

Serve Quarterly

In your small group, don't forget about others. Serving is a vital part of the health of a small group. And if you don't plan for it, it won't happen. We've talked about the importance of everyone in a small group bringing their gifts to the table. Let's do that here, too. Encourage someone to step up and be the group's "service coordinator" or "outreach director." That person should be constantly looking for ways to get the group off of the couch and into the community.

It is fine to serve by yourself, but it is better to serve with your group. If you oversee all of the small groups in your local church, get together a list of opportunities for groups to utilize. Tap into the organizations your church supports, and contact them. Ask them if there are a few different tasks a group could knock out on a regular basis. Or gather a list of families that could use some help, and brainstorm some projects that could be completed by a small group. Or help group leaders dream about what their group could do based on their location.

Serving generously builds community. You don't have to do it quarterly. Feel free to serve more often. Just be sure to serve. Help your group give of themselves generously and regularly. Finding something to do outside the walls of your church building and outside the walls of your home is a good rhythm to build, because it's sustainable. And it'll make a bigger impact than you could imagine.

Put Me In, Coach

I remember a few years back talking with a small groups pastor. I often do that because I'm convinced I don't have all of the answers, all of the angles, all of the good ideas, or all of the solutions. I've made it a habit to learn from anyone anywhere, no matter the size church they lead, how long they've been in ministry, or what model they employ. One question I always ask is, "What would you say is the most important thing for a groups pastor to get a handle on?" Without even a breath of hesitation, he said, "Coaching. If you don't figure it out now, it'll have disastrous consequences the more you move forward."

When a group leader feels cared for, they will lead better. It's a simple principle, but one that's overlooked by so many. Group leaders don't have to have a weekly meeting with their coach in order to be successful. They just need to know that they're cared for, loved, and supported.

Coaching is much less about information and much more about relationship. Information is important, but not nearly as much about the relational side of things. Because if you don't have a relationship with a group leader you're coaching:

1. They won't come to you when things fall apart.

2. The information you share will be cold and lifeless.

The #1 goal of a coach is to focus on the health of the leader. Nearly every time, if the group leader is healthy spiritually, the group is healthy spiritually. Which makes group leader health a significant thing to focus on. So what does this health look like?

A "healthy" small group is one that accomplishes "the win" for your system, which means that a healthy group at our church may look a little different than the one at your church. And that's ok. The first step is defining "the win." For us, the goal of every small group, no matter when or where they meet, whether they're comprised of singles, couples, senior adults, or just-out-of-college, every group has the same goal: to take a step of faith together.

In fact, with every training we offer, we make it clear: "It's important to know what the win is for your small group. And that win is taking steps of faith together."

Typically during our new leaders training, we'll brainstorm what a "step of faith" looks like, so that along the journey of their small group, a group leader can celebrate these small wins that contribute to the overall win for their group. What are these wins?

- Reading the Bible
- Getting baptized
- Engaging in small group
- Showing up consistently
- Choosing to obey God with a certain area of their life that they'd not before

What gets celebrated gets replicated. A good group leader looks for these wins, even in small ways, and celebrates them. They point them out publicly, in front of the group, and let the group know that every step of faith in the right direction is worth celebrating.

Sometimes a small step reminds us that 100, or 1000 more small steps need to be taken. One Sunday when my son was two, he ran up and down the halls of our church building (a high school, in fact) yelling, "Pee pee! Pee pee!" We were in the middle of one of the most fun stages of parenting: potty training. I could've gotten frustrated. Embarrassed. Angry. Or indifferent. But I was none of that. I chose to laugh. Why? Because it's funny! My two year-old son is telling the whole world that he just peed in the toilet, not his pants. Was it embarrassing? Yep. Was it frustrating, especially because he also peed in his diaper? Yep. But in that moment, I chose not to focus on the growth that still needed to happen. I chose to celebrate with my son.

And we would do well to remind ourselves that our Father rejoices over even a small step of faith. Good fathers don't punish their children when they pee in their diaper, even though they're learning not to. I don't scold my son, even though I've told him countless times that he's supposed to pee in the toilet. I have the future in mind. I know that, at some point, the battle with this will be over. We'll work through this. It is just a step in his journey towards maturity. He'll mature out of it, and in the meantime, I'm going to celebrate small steps in the right direction.

And I can't help but think that God has the future in mind with us too. He has the bigger picture of our growth and maturity in mind at all times. And yes, at times, we need discipline. But He celebrates small steps in the right direction because He can see what we cannot. And while we're sitting in our own guilt and shame, God's seeing the future, and is ready to offer us grace if we'll just step towards Him.

Everyone Brings Something

Another key component to leading an effective

group is <u>sharing ministry</u>. Allow others in the group to lead the worship time, lead the study, bring refreshments, and host the group. <u>Cultivating group ownership is important if members are going to feel needed and appreciated</u>. It also helps to keep you from burning out or from thinking that you can do it all yourself (Ephesians 4:12). <u>Develop contributors, not customers.</u>

In order to facilitate this development, you need to designate people having authority in your group. There are a few things that need to happen in order for a group to be successful. Assign them to individuals in your group.

- Hosting: someone to coordinate the rotation of homes
- Prayer requests: someone to distribute them via email
- Food schedule: someone to make sure the meal happens
- Serving schedule: an outreach coordinator for quarterly service projects
- Fun weeks: someone to make sure the group keeps laughing

The Health of the Leader

<u>The health of a small group starts with the health of the small group leader</u>. If the group leader isn't

growing, you can forget about the small group growing.

If you want to gauge the health of the group, put the thermometer in the group leader's mouth. Think about it with me.

- If the group leader is not being honest, why would the group be compelled to honesty?
- If the group leader is not living life in integrity, why would the group be compelled to integrity?
- If the group leader is not spending time with God regularly, how can she lead others spiritually?
- If the group leader is not exercising his prayer life, does he really believe prayer works?

The book of James reminds us of the gravity of this ministry: "Not many of you should become teachers, my fellow believers, because you know that we who teach will be judged more strictly" (James 3:1). Why? Because those who are teaching will be judged not just for their own lives but for how their followers lived. If a group leader's marriage is struggling, you can bet that the group is suffering. If a group leader is hiding a secret sin, you can bet that the group is suffering. If a group leader is not living self-sacrificially, you can bet the group isn't valuing that ether. How can you make a disciple if you're not becoming one yourself?

When I sit down with a group leader to talk about their group, I don't just focus on group dynamics. I zoom in on how they're growing. How their marriage looks. How they're maintaining influence with people who have yet to follow Jesus. A healthy shepherd will have healthy sheep. Or at the very least, a healthy shepherd will know how to lead his sheep towards better health.

The health of the leaders is critical for a healthy group. When a group leader loses sight of the goal, the people in the group get off target. When the group leader strays, the group tends to wander. No group can thrive under poor leadership. If you are a group leader, then the first step in having a healthy group is making sure you are spiritually prepared and equipped. All of the tips in this book will not work well if you are not seeking God's will.

You may love to teach. You may love to lead. You may love to show hospitality. Apart from Christ working in your life, though, these loves become selfish endeavors. Your group is not meant to serve your desires. You are to lead your group to serve Christ. Humility is how a group will thrive. Now get to it. Go start that small group.

Questions:

How would you define "health" for a small group? What does a healthy group do?

Have you been in a healthy small group before? How is your life marked because of that experience?

Do you have a plan for coaching and shepherding small group leaders? Who do you have in mind that could be a small group coach?

If it's true that you can't make a disciple if you're not becoming one, how do you know that you're becoming a disciple?

Is fun a part of your small group strategy? How do you plan on building fun into your group experience?